Tunes and studies for the trumpet

Book 1

PREFACE

This book has been planned to supply elementary material for the beginner of all ages. The tunes and studies develop steadily, and one or two can be mastered each week over a period of a year to eighteen months. They have been devised to give musical satisfaction, as well as providing a serious basis for technical development.

No space has been wasted on rudiments of music: the book concentrates on material which will teach the student how to play his instrument. The explanatory notes have been kept as short as possible, and the student should seek some professional tuition and advice, especially in the early stages of playing. Bad faults in note production and embouchure are often difficult to rectify once they get a hold.

This collection can be used by beginners on any brass instrument playing in the treble clef, except the French horn.

I would like to thank my many friends and colleagues who have made suggestions for this book, and also, in discussion and argument over the years, have assisted in bringing the ideas enclosed to fruition.

Bram Wiggins

Tunes and studies for the trumpet, Book 2 is also available.

© Oxford University Press 1970

Oxford University Press

Music Department, Walton Street, Oxford OX2 6DP   Printed in Great Britain

INTRODUCTION

The trumpet is a transposing instrument. The instrument in general use, and on which the majority of students learn to play, is that pitched in B♭. This means that the lowest note that can be played on the open tube, using no valves, sounds the note B♭ and its harmonic series.

We read the note C ♮ and the sound produced is B♭ ♮. On the C trumpet we read C and the sound is C. This system is used so that a player can play an instrument in any pitch and use the same fingering for the notes he reads on the part.

In the orchestra, trumpets are used pitched in B♭, C, D, E♭, and F, and sometimes a high B♭ instrument is used, pitched an octave above the common B♭. Orchestral players usually transpose the parts written for A, C, D, E♭, E, F, and sometimes G trumpet, using the B♭ or C instrument, the smaller trumpets being used only for specialized works. The A trumpet and cornet were at one time very popular, but are now practically obsolete.

Holding the Instrument. It is essential that the student holds the trumpet correctly from the first lesson. The weight of the instrument is taken solely by the left hand, leaving the right hand free to manipulate the valves. The L.H. thumb should be on the mouthpiece side of the 1st valve casing, and the fingers around the 3rd valve casing, using the 3rd or 4th fingers to work the mobile 3rd slide, if this useful gadget is fitted to the instrument. The valves must be as perpendic-ular as possible so that they go straight down.

The right thumb should be placed under the mouthpipe between the 1st and 2nd : valve casing, and the little finger *must* be in the hook provided for it. The fingers are then in the correct position to work the valves, and should be slightly 'clawed', not straight. The elbows should be away from the sides to allow the rib cage freedom to expand while breathing. If this position is insisted on the student holds the instrument in a comfortable and balanced way, and the possi-bility of damaging the valve action by incorrect fingering is eliminated.

Producing sound. In order to do this, the lips are vibrated by forcing an even column of air through them into the mouthpiece. The tip of the tongue must be used behind the upper teeth to commence this vibration, with an action as though articulating the syllable 'TU'. The student must realize that the tongue does not 'spit' the notes, but acts as valve which when drawn back releases the air column. Before trying to sound the trumpet, try tonguing on the mouthpiece alone. The lip muscles are drawn tighter together to produce higher notes, so that the air is directed through a smaller aperture, and relaxed for the lower notes. The lips should not be stretched back in a smiling position for the higher notes, as is taught occasionally in older methods, but should be tightened by bunching or 'puckering' the muscles together.

Always start a practice session by playing a series of long notes in the middle register, not too loudly at first. This 'warms up' the facial muscles, as well as warming the tube of the instrument. This should become a daily routine, regardless of the degree of efficiency that the student eventually attains. Develop the habit of listening critically to every note played, whether in practice or performance, and do not practise any study at a faster tempo than is comfortably possible. The tempo should be set at the speed you can play the most difficult passage, and no faster.

Set a tempo and keep to it. It is a sensible idea to have a planned practice routine, covering all the different aspects of trumpet playing in a concentrated form. Never practise too long without a break, for besides physical fatigue, the concentration may flag. Little and often is better than overdoing it in one long stint.

The Mouthpiece. The choice of the mouthpiece is very important, and, if possible, the advice of an experienced player should be sought before purchasing one. What is suitable for one player is not necessarily right for another. But the very small, shallow-cupped, wide-rimmed type of mouthpiece should be avoided at all costs, as the sound tends to be thin and shrill, the lower notes are often difficult to produce, and what little advantage may be experienced in the upper register at first is lost as the player becomes accustomed to it. Most reputable makers supply good, sensible models with their instruments. A fairly deep cup with a flattish, not-too-wide rim is recommended. (Vincent Bach models, Nos: 6-1, no shallower than a 'C' cup). Always keep the back-bore clean, a small brush or a pipe cleaner being ideal for this purpose.

Care of the Instrument. The instrument should be rinsed through weekly with warm, not hot, water, and the mouthpipe cleaned with a brush or pull-through. Valves should be regularly oiled with makers' prepared valve oil, preferably of a thin texture, wiping off all the old oil before applying new, and the slides must be kept greased.

Most instruments are now fitted with a mobile 3rd slide to correct the tuning of certain sharp notes, notably the low D and D♭ (C♯). The student should learn to use this device right from the start.

Breathing. There are many theories regarding breathing when playing brass instruments, which can be considered and studied at a later stage. At the beginning breathe naturally and deeply, using the diaphragm to control both inhalation and exhalation, and take the air in through the sides of the mouth. Do not raise the shoulders when taking a breath (a common fault with the beginner), and keep the arms away from the sides so that the movement of the chest is not restricted.

Fingering Chart for the Trumpet or Cornet

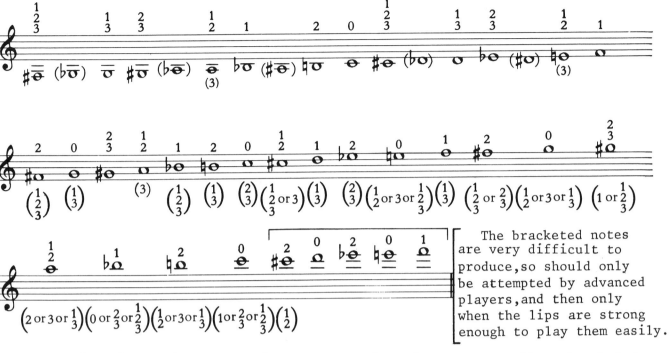

The bracketed notes are very difficult to produce, so should only be attempted by advanced players, and then only when the lips are strong enough to play them easily.

The fingerings written over the notes are those in common use, those bracketed underneath are alternative fingerings, used occasionally to facilitate technical passages, adjust tuning, trilling, etc.

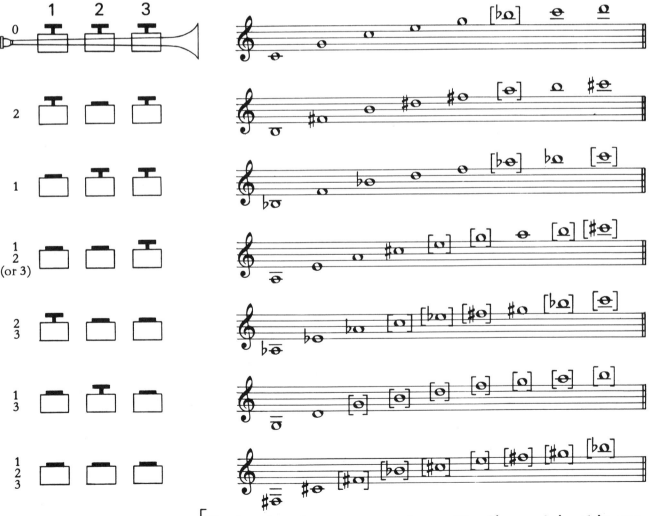

The bracketed notes are not usually fingered in this way.

The beginner must learn to sustain and control the sounds on the instrument, and must therefore practise long notes. Stress has been put on this in all the early studies. Long-note practice develops breathing, control, and good sound.

In No. 1 count 4 slowly on each note and bar of rest, and repeat every two bars at least three times before proceeding to the next note. Make sure each note is attacked (tongued) and released cleanly. To stop the sound it is necessary only to discontinue blowing, and no action of the tongue is required.

This study should be practised at a level forte, with a full, sustained sound, with a crescendo and diminuendo ($p<f>p$), and vice-versa ($f>p<f$). Always blow *through* the instrument, not into it.

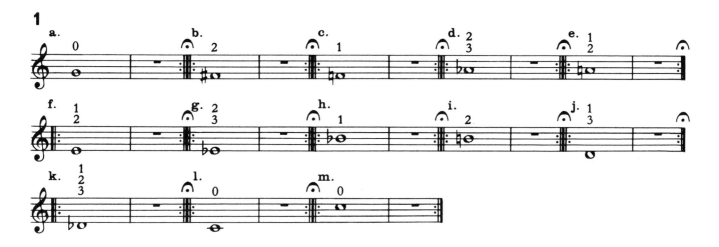

This study and Nos. 2-5 should also be practised using the following rhythms instead of semibreves (whole notes).

In the early stages of playing some students will be able to produce the notes G downwards, while others will play upwards to C. In the first case series 'a' should be practised first, and in the second case series 'b'. If the student plays C to C with equal ease, Nos. 2-5 should be worked in the order written. Still count slowly and don't forget the rests. Try to observe the dynamic markings, but *do not blow too loud.*

1

3

4

5

In No. 6 the notes are changed without any assistance from the valves, so the lips have to do all the work by tightening or relaxing. Note that for this exercise G is sometimes played $\frac{1}{3}$ and F♯ $\frac{1}{3}$ (G♭).

6

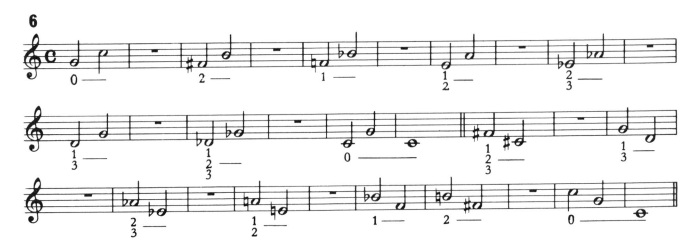

7

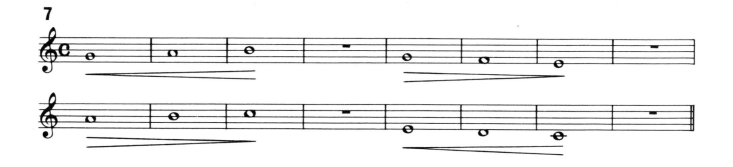

8 Chorale

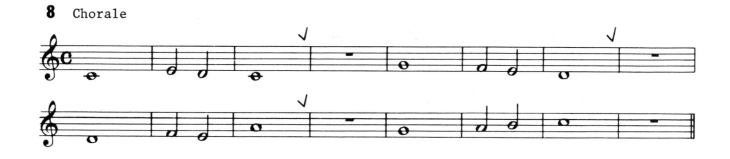

9 Solemn Flourish

10 Lament

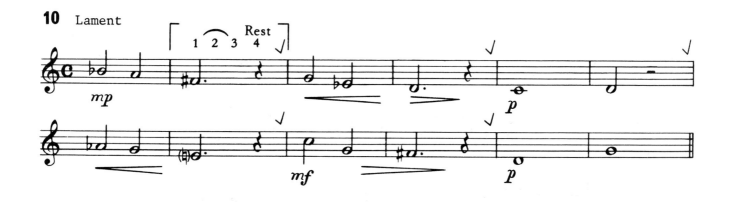

In No. 11 we dispense with rests at the end of phrases, so breaths should be taken as marked (✓). It is most important that breaths are taken in the correct places (i.e. at the end of phrases), or the sense of the music is destroyed.

11 French Folk Tune

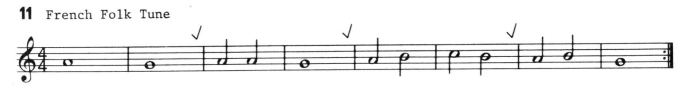

12

13 Tallis' Canon

14 The Old Hundredth

Try to play this tune without taking a breath where the tick is in brackets.

15 Waltz

In No. 16 crotchets (quarter notes) are introduced. Make sure each note is tongued cleanly, and that the long notes are given their full value. Do not play too fast.

19 German Folk Tune

20 Czech Folk Tune

21 The Carman's Whistle (William Byrd)

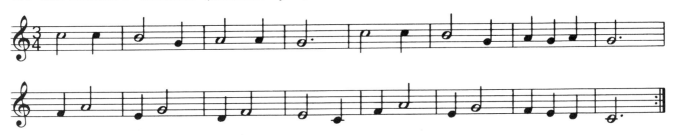

22 Theme from the 'Surprise Symphony' (Haydn)

23 Minuet (Arne)

24

25 Jubilate (Old Russian Hymn)

26 Sicilian Melody

In No. 27 some notes are joined by a slur (⌒). Notes joined in this way are not articulated after the initial attack. Move the valves quickly while keeping the air moving through the tube. (See note to No. 36).

27 Rousseau's Dream

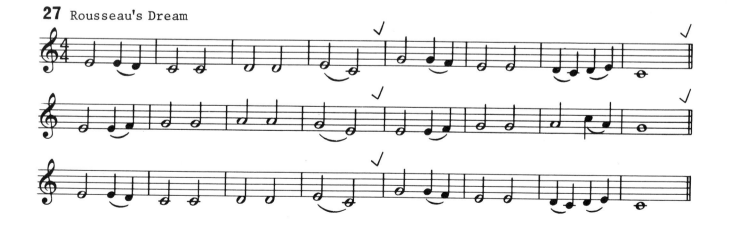

Practise No. 28 as No. 1. Do not progress to a higher note until it can be produced with comfort and without effort. Never force or strain for high notes. The range will increase naturally as the muscles strengthen with regular practice. To produce the lower notes the jaw should be protruded slightly.

28 Extending the range

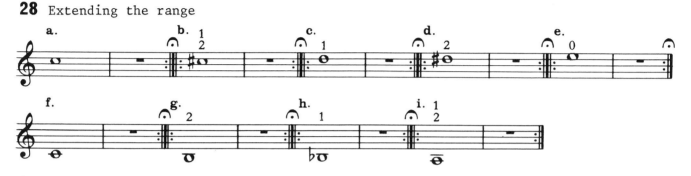

29 C major scale and arpeggio *(All scales and arpeggios must be memorised)*

30 A minor melodic scale and arpeggio

A minor harmonic scale

31 Study in C major

Alla marcia

32 Study in A minor

Lento

33 Puer Nobis (15th Century Carol)

34 Pavana (Delibes)

35 March for Clarions

Allegro ma non troppo

> *This sign is an accent, and notes so marked must be tongued harder.*

9

No. 36. When slurring from one note to another, the initial note must be tongued, and the air stream continued through the note change. When moving from one note to another, the valves must always be put down or let up quickly, whether the music is fast or slow, or the change will not be clean. When two or more valves are used simultaneously they must move together, not after each other. This is even more essential when slurring.

36 Slurring Study

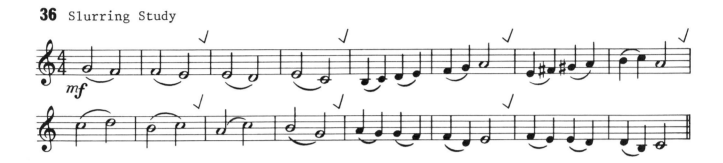

No. 37 introduces quavers (eighth notes). There are two quavers to each beat so count 'one *and* two *and*' carefully as marked, and make certain the notes are cleanly tongued and equal in length and volume. Make sure that the tongue and fingers always work together.

37

38

39

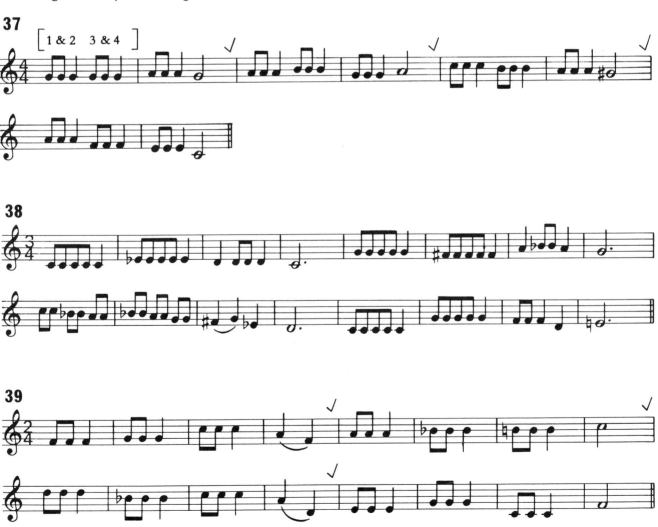

40 Goe from my Window (Old English)

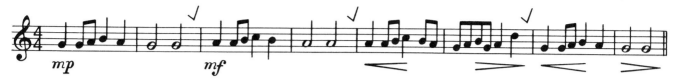

41 The Quail (French Folk Song)

Andantino

42 Hungarian Folk Song

43

44

45 *Be careful to differentiate between slurred and tongued notes.*

46 Menuet (Michiel Parent)

47 My Love's an Arbutus (Irish Folk Song)

48 Allegro (Telemann)

49 Extending the range

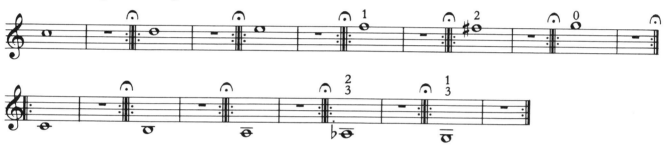

50 F major scale and arpeggio

51 D minor melodic scale and arpeggio

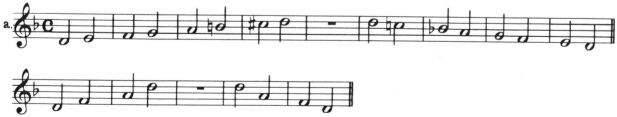

D minor harmonic scale

No. 52 is designed to strengthen the facial and lip muscles, and the slurs
have to be made without the assistance of any change of valve. When slurring
upwards the lip muscles are tightened and the back of the tongue should be raised,
as though making the sounds 'AAHH-EEEE'. Play this study very slowly, and use
the alternative fingerings as marked. Relax in the rest bars.

52 Slurring study *(use fingerings as marked)*

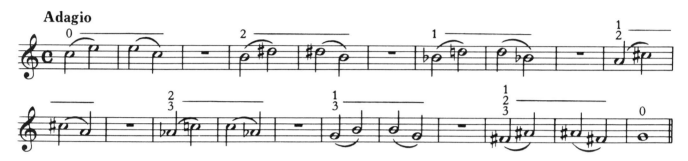

Study No.6 can now be practised slurred instead of tongued.

In No. 53 be careful to give the tenuto (-) notes their full value and make the
staccato notes (.) short.

53 Study in F major

No. 54 is in ⁶⁄₈ time (compound time), and here the beat is a dotted crotchet,
which is divided into threes instead of twos as in previous studies.

54 Study in D minor

If No. 55 is found to be too strenuous to play complete, it should be practised in two separate sections (as marked a and b).

55 Minuett from the 'Royal Fireworks Music' (Handel)

Allegro marziale

56 Minuet (J.S.Bach)

Moderato

No. 57 should be played very smoothly, so attention must be paid to clean, smooth fingering. It is advisable to practise slowly at first, and gradually work the study up to tempo, as the student becomes more conversant with it.

57 Chromatic Study

58 Dotted crotchets, followed by quaver

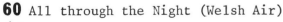

59

60 All through the Night (Welsh Air)

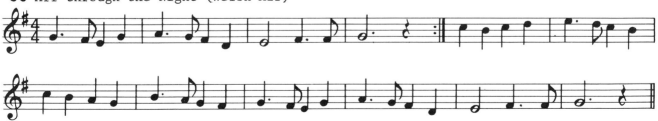

16

61 Trumpet Processional

62 G major scale and arpeggio

63 E minor melodic scale and arpeggio

E minor harmonic scale

64 Study in G major

Allegretto

In No. 65 the beat is divided by a jerky rhythm ♪♪ [♪♪♪] . Make certain that the semiquaver (sixteenth note) is always short enough, as often this rhythm is played incorrectly in a lazy fashion (ie. ♩♪ instead of ♪♪). It must be crisp and martial.

65 Study in E minor

Tempo di marcia

66 Austrian Carol

67 David of the White Rock (Welsh Tune)

68 Captain Morgan's March (Welsh Air)

69 Figaro's Aria (Mozart)

70 A Study and Tune in compound time

71 A Trumpet Air (18th Century)

72 Slurring study *(use fingerings marked)*

The bracketed notes in No. 73 are probably above the range of the student at this stage of his development, so should be omitted unless they can be produced with ease.

73 B♭ major scale and arpeggio

74 G minor melodic scale and arpeggio

a.

G minor harmonic scale

b.

The rhythm ♪.♪♪ is often played incorrectly, and it may help the student to sing the word AM-STER-DAM to it before playing No. 75 and to think this while playing.

75 Study in B♭ major

No. 76 is not as easy as it may look. It should be lyrical in style, and some thought should be given to interpretation and phrasing. Make sure the slurs are always clean and smooth. Think and listen.

76 Study in G minor

77 Westering Home (Scottish Folk Dance)

78 Gavotte (J.S.Bach)

79 Chromatic Study

Allegro ma non troppo

The single tongue is very often neglected, although it is one of the most important assets of good trumpet playing. Double and triple tonguing should never be used to replace the single tongue except in phrases which are too fast for clean articulation. No. 80, and similar studies, can and should be used as daily practice routines.

80 Tonguing Study

81 Legato Study

82 Trumpet Tune (Purcell)

A trill is introduced at the end of the first stanza of No. 83. It should be practised alone, before being inserted into the tune, making sure that the notes are even. Take care that the valves always go right down and up again. A trill should be played from a long tube to a short tube when possible, so often it is advisable to use alternative fingerings to ensure the natural sharpening of the tube (i.e. when trilling from E to F E should be played ¹₂).

83 A Trumpet Tune 'The Duke of Marlborough's March' (Jeremiah Clarke)

Allegro marziale

In No. 84 each bar should be repeated at least four times, and should, at first, be practised slowly. Make sure that each phrase is even. These exercises are planned to develop the independence of the fingers, especially the naturally weak third finger, and should become daily routine practice.

84 Fingering Exercises

85 D major scale and arpeggio

86 B minor melodic scale and arpeggio

B minor harmonic scale

87 Study in D major

Allegretto

27

No. 88 may be found difficult at first, so practise slowly to begin with, but always play rhythmically. Note the F double sharp (x) in bar 10.

88 Study in B minor

89 Gaudeamus Igitur (Student Song)

90 The Trout (Schubert)

91 Solveig's Song (Grieg)

Andante con espress.

mp

rall. *a tempo* *rall.*

92

f

   In No. 93 two new notes are introduced, G♯ and A. If these notes prove to be too high play E for G♯ and F for A. Never strain to play, or force, high notes, as irreparable harm can be caused. As the muscles strengthen with use and practice, the range will develop and extend naturally.

93 Sarabande (Corelli)

94 The Blackbird (Welsh Air)

95 Scandinavian Folk Song

96 The Birdcatcher's Song from 'The Magic Flute' (Mozart)

The student may experience a slight soreness at the root of the tongue during the practice of No. 97 and similar studies, as more or less dormant muscles are being used and exercised. All muscles must be fatigued to strengthen them.

97 Tonguing Study

98 Study in Lyrical Style (Aria)

Andante cantabile

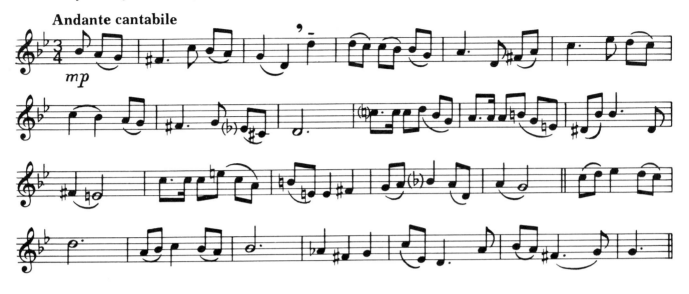

mp

99 Interval Study

Tempo di menuetto

f

simile

Fine

D.C.

32

100 Slurring Study

101 My Heart, Ever Faithful (J.S. Bach)

33

102 The Lass with the Delicate Air (Michael Arne)

103 Silent Worship (Handel)

104 Sellinger's Round (Old English 16th Century)

105 Minuet (Jeremiah Clarke)

Allegretto

106 Trumpet Tune (John Stanley)

Reproduced and printed by
Halstan & Co. Ltd., Amersham, Bucks., England